US STATES AND THEIR CAPITALS

Geography 2nd Grade for Kids

Children's Earth Sciences Books Edition

SPEEDY
PUBLISHING

Speedy Publishing LLC

40 E. Main St. #1156

Newark, DE 19711

www.speedypublishing.com

United States of America is a federal republic composed of 50 States. Since 1800 Washington DC has been the Capital of the United States. This book will let you know the different capitals of each 50 states.

Alabama

Alaska

Arizona

Alabama is the 30th-most extensive and the 24th-most populous of the 50 United States. It became the 22nd state on December 14, 1819. The first rocket put to moon was built there. Its Capital City is Montgomery.

Alaska was first discovered in 1741 when Danish explorer Vitus Jonassen Bering sighted it on a voyage from Siberia. Alaska officially became the 49th state on January 3, 1959. Its Capital City is Juneau.

Arizona It is the 6th largest and the 14th most populous of the 50 states. The home of the Grand Canyon National Park. Its capital and largest city is Phoenix..

Arkansas

California

Colorado

Arkansas   the 33rd most populous of the 50 United States. It is the 25th state on June 15, 1836. The capital and most populous city is Little Rock.

California is the most populous U.S. state and the third largest state by area after Alaska and Texas. Its capital City is Sacramento.

Colorado is the 8th most extensive and the 22nd most populous of the 50 United States. The United States Air Force Academy is located in Colorado Springs. Its capital city is Denver.

Connecticut

Delaware

Florida

Connecticut is known as the "Constitution State", the "Nutmeg State", the "Provisions State", and the "Land of Steady Habits". The third smallest state by area. The capital city is Hartford.

Delaware was the first state to ratify the United States constitution. The second smallest, the sixth least populous, but the sixth most densely populated of the 50 United States. Its capital City is Dover.

Florida is the 22nd most extensive, the 3rd most populous and the 8th most densely populated of the United States. The first bank automated teller machine especially for rollerbladers was installed in Miami. Its capital city is Tallahassee

Georgia

Hawaii

Idaho

Georgia was named for King George II of England. The 24th largest and the 8th most populous of the 50 United States. The third smallest state by area. The capital city is Atlanta.

Hawaii is the 50th state in U.S. The only state located in Oceania and the only one composed entirely of islands. Its capital City is Honolulu.

Idaho is the 14th largest, the 39th most populous, and the 7th least densely populated of the 50 United States. Post Falls is known as Idaho's River City. Its capital city is Boise.

Illinois

Indiana

Iowa

Illinois is the 5th most populous state and 25th largest state in terms of land area. Peoria is the oldest community in Illinois. The largest city is Chicago and the capital city is Springfield.

Indiana is the 38th largest by area and the 16th most populous of the 50 United States. President Abraham Lincoln moved and spent his boyhood in Spencer County, Indiana. Its capital City is Indianapolis.

Iowa is the 26th largest in land area and the 30th most populous of the 50 United States. Scranton is home to Iowa's oldest water tower still in service. Its capital city is Des Moines.

Kansas

Kentucky

Louisiana

Kansas is the 15th largest by area and the 34th most populous of the 50 United States. Named after the Kansa Native American tribe. The largest city is Wichita and the capital city is Topeka.

Kentucky is the 37st largest in land area and the 26th most populous of the 50 United States. Known as the "Bluegrass State", a nickname based on the bluegrass found in many of its pastures due to the fertile soil. Its capital City is Frankfort.

Louisiana is the 31st largest in land area and the 25th most populous of the 50 United States. Louisiana was named in honor of King Louis XIV. Its capital city is Baton Rouge.

Maine

Maryland

Massachusetts

Maine is the 39th largest by area and the 42nd most populous of the 50 United States. Maine's earliest inhabitants were descendants of Ice Age hunters. The capital city is Augusta.

Maryland is one of the smallest states in terms of area, as well as one of the most densely populated. The state considered to be the birthplace of religious freedom in America. Its capital City is Annapolis.

Massachusetts is the 7th smallest state by land area, but the 15th most populous and the 3rd most densely populated of the 50 states. The first subway system in the United States was built in Boston, Massachusetts on 1897. Its capital city is Baton Rouge.

Michigan

Minnesota

Mississippi

Michigan is the 11th largest by area and the 10th most populous of the 50 United States. Detroit is known as the car capital of the world. The largest City is Detroit and the capital city is Lansing.

Minnesota is the 12th largest by area and the 21st most populous of the 50 United States. Its name comes from the Dakota word for "clear blue water". Its capital City is Saint Paul.

Mississippi is the 32nd largest by land area same rank as the most populous of the 50 states. The world's largest cactus plantation is in Edwards, Mississippi. Its capital city is Jackson.

Missouri

Montana

Nebraska

Missouri is the 21st largest by area and the 18th most populous of the 50 United States. It is known as the "Show Me State". The capital city is Jefferson City.

Montana is the 4th largest by area and the 44th most populous of the 50 United States. No state has as many different species of mammals as Montana. Its capital City is Helena.

Nebraska is the 16th largest by land area same rank 37th as the most populous of the 50 states. Nebraska was once called "The Great American Desert". Its capital city is Lincoln.

Nevada

New Hampshire

New Jersey

Nevada is the 7th largest by area and the 35th most populous of the 50 United States. The largest gold-producing state in the nation. It is second in the world behind South Africa. The capital city is Carson City.

New Hampshire is the 46th largest by area and the 41st most populous of the 50 United States. The first capital city of New Hampshire was in Exeter. Its capital City is Concord.

New Jersey is the 47th largest by land area same rank 11th as the most populous of the 50 states. The only state where all its counties are classified as metropolitan areas. Its largest City is Newark and capital city is Trenton.

New Mexico

New York

North Carolina

New Mexico is the 5th largest by area and the 36th most populous of the 50 United States. Santa Fe is the highest capital city in the United States at 7,000 feet above sea level. The capital city is Santa Fe.

New York is the 27th largest by area and the 4th most populous of the 50 United States. Known as "The Big Apple" a term coined by musicians meaning to play the big time. Its capital City is Albany.

North Carolina is the 27th largest by land area and the 9th most populous of the 50 United States. The first state owned art museum in the country is located in Raleigh. The capital city is Raleigh.

North Dakota

Ohio

Oklahoma

North Dakota is the 19th largest by area and the 47th most populous of the 50 United States. Milk is the official state beverage. The capital city is Bismarck.

Ohio is the 34th largest by area and the 7th most populous of the 50 United States. Ohio is the leading producer of greenhouse and nursery plants. Its capital City is Columbus.

Oklahoma is the 20th largest by land area and the 28th most populous of the 50 United States. An Oklahoman, Sylvan Goldman, invented the first shopping cart. The capital city is Oklahoma City.

Oregon

Pennsylvania

Rhode Island

Oregon is the 9th largest by area and the 26th most populous of the 50 United States. Oregon has more ghost towns than any other state. The capital city is Salem.

Pennsylvania is the 33rd largest by area and the 6th most populous of the 50 United States. Hershey is considered the Chocolate Capital of the United States. Its capital City is Harrisburg.

Rhode Island is the 50th largest by land area and the 43th most populous of the 50 United States. The last of the original thirteen colonies to become a state. The capital city is Providence.

South Carolina

South Dakota

Tennessee

South Carolina is the 40th largest by area and the 23rd most populous of the 50 United States. South Carolina entered the Union on May 23, 1788 and became the 8th state. The capital city is Columbia.

South Dakota is the 17th largest by area and the 46th most populous of the 50 United States. The faces of George Washington, Thomas Jefferson, Theodore Roosevelt, and Abraham Lincoln are sculpted into Mount Rushmore the world's greatest mountain carving in the U.S. Its capital City is Pierre.

Tennessee is the 36th largest by land area and the 17th most populous of the 50 United States. Tennessee has more than 3,800 documented caves. The capital city is Nashville.

Texas

Utah

Vermont

Texas is the 2nd largest by area and same rank as the most populous of the 50 United States. Texas is popularly known as The Lone Star State. The capital city is Austin.

Utah is the 13th largest by area and the 31st most populous of the 50 United States. The name Utah comes from the Native American Ute tribe and means people of the mountains. Its capital City is Salt Lake City.

Vermont is the 45th largest by land area and the 49th most populous of the 50 United States. Until 1996, Vermont was the only state without a Wal-Mart. The capital city is Montpelier.

Virginia

Washington

West Virginia

Virginia is the 35th largest by area and 12th most populous of the 50 United States. Virginia was named for England's "Virgin Queen," Elizabeth I. The capital city is Richmond.

Washington is the 18th largest by area and 13th most populous of the 50 United States. The state of Washington is the only state to be named after a United States president. The capital city is Olympia.

West Virginia is the 41st largest by area and the 38th most populous of the 50 United States. Mother's Day was first observed at Andrews Church in Grafton on May 10, 1908. Its capital City is Charleston.

Wisconsin

Wyoming

Wisconsin

Wisconsin is the 23rd largest by land area and the 20th most populous of the 50 United States. The state is nicknamed the Badger State. The capital city is Madison.

Wyoming is the 10th largest by area and 50th most populous of the 50 United States. Wyoming was the first state to give women the right to vote. The capital city is Cheyenne.

BONUS TRIVIA

Did You know that the United States of America acquired Alaska From Russia in the year 1865?

Visit

BABY PROFESSOR
EDUCATION KIDS

www.BabyProfessorBooks.com

to download Free Baby Professor eBooks
and view our catalog of new and exciting
Children's Books

CPSIA information can be obtained
at www.ICGtesting.com
Printed in the USA
BVHW010217110121
597532BV00029B/464

9 781683 055228